Science Inquiry

HOW DO
PUSHES AND PULLS
AFFECT MOTION?

T0081090

by Lisa M. Bolt Simons

PEBBLE
a capstone imprint

Published by Pebble, an imprint of Capstone.
1710 Roe Crest Drive, North Mankato, Minnesota 56003
capstonepub.com

Library of Congress Cataloging-in-Publication Data
Names: Bolt Simons, Lisa M., 1969- author.
Title: How do pushes and pulls affect motion? / Lisa M. Bolt Simons.
Description: North Mankato, Minnesota : Pebble, [2022] | Series: Science inquiry | Includes bibliographical references and index. | Audience: Ages 5-8 | Audience: Grades K-1 | Summary: "You push your friend while they swing. You pull open a door. What happens when you push or pull an object? Let's investigate pushing and pulling forces!"— Provided by publisher.
Identifiers: LCCN 2021029724 (print) | LCCN 2021029725 (ebook) | ISBN 9781663970329 (hardcover) | ISBN 9781666324914 (paperback) | ISBN 9781666324921 (pdf) | ISBN 9781666324945 (kindle edition)
Subjects: LCSH: Force and energy—Juvenile literature. | Force and energy—Experiments—Juvenile literature.
Classification: LCC QC73.4 .B65 2022 (print) | LCC QC73.4 (ebook) | DDC 531/.6—dc23
LC record available at https://lccn.loc.gov/2021029724
LC ebook record available at https://lccn.loc.gov/2021029725

Image Credits
Capstone Studio: Karon Dubke, 5, 7 (Top Left and Right); Dreamstime: Sasi Ponchaisang, 18; Getty Images: ImagesBazaar, Cover (Left), John D. Buffington, Cover (Right); Shutterstock: balabolka, Cover (Design Elements), elinaxx1v, 22, fizkes, 13, Monkey Business Images, 1, 7 (Bottom Left), 21, 29, Pascalis PW, 7 (Bottom Right), Pressmaster, 15, Purino, 9, Robert Kneschke, 24, Romrodphoto, 19, Samuel Borges Photography, 26, Sergey Novikov, 8, 25, Slatan, 10, TuktaBaby, 11, wavebreakmedia, 16

Editorial Credits
Editor: Erika L. Shores; Designer: Dina Her; Media Researcher: Jo Miller; Production Specialist: Tori Abraham

All internet sites appearing in back matter were available and accurate when this book was sent to press.

TABLE OF CONTENTS

Words in **bold** are in the glossary.

A PUSH AND PULL INVESTIGATION

You're at the park. You sit on a swing but don't move. You ask a friend to push you. Maybe you want one push. Maybe you want several pushes.

As long as your friend pushes you, the swing changes **position**. Now you have **motion**. You and the swing are moving. When you're done swinging, you drag your toes. The motion stops.

A swing needs a push to start motion. A swing needs something to stop the motion. How do other objects get motion? How do other objects stop motion?

Let's do an **investigation**. Look at the photos on page 7. The person in each photo is moving something.

On a piece of paper, draw a line down the middle. On one side write, "How the object moves." On the other side write, "How the object stops."

Make **observations**. Gather information. How do you open a door? How do you close a door? How do you move a bike? How do you stop a bike from moving? How do you move a cart? How do you stop the cart?

WHAT IS FORCE?

Pushes and pulls are two types of **forces**. A force gives an object motion from where it's resting.

To push is to move an object away from you. To pull is to bring an object toward you. An object can start moving if it's pushed or pulled. An object can stop moving if the pushing or pulling stops. An object can also stop moving if it is pushed or pulled in the opposite direction.

Gravity is another kind of force. But it's a force that doesn't need anyone touching it. Gravity pulls everything down toward Earth.

Apples grow on trees. When they are ripe, they fall to the ground. No one has to pull them off and throw them on the ground. When they fall off the branch, they do not float.

Kids play on the monkey bars.
If a kid slips, they will fall. Gravity
pulls the kid to Earth.

Friction is also a force. This force opposes, or tries to stop, motion when two objects are touching.

Think about pushing a heavy box over thick carpet. The carpet pushes against the box. This creates friction as you push the box. The box is hard to move.

What happens if you push a heavy box on a smooth wood floor? The box moves easily and quickly over the floor. There is a lot less friction between the box and the smooth floor.

HOW DOES STRENGTH AFFECT PUSHES AND PULLS?

There are other things that affect motion besides force. Strength can affect motion too. What if your friend gives you a gentle push on a swing? You probably won't move much. If your friend gives you a strong push, you will swing higher.

The strength of the push can also affect **distance**. If you kick a ball softly, it won't go far. If you kick a ball hard, it will go farther.

Strength is the same for pulling. If you pull harder, the object will go farther.

What happens during tug-of-war? Two sides pull a rope in opposite directions. One group tries to move the other group across a center line. If one side is stronger, it will pull the other group to its side.

Distance is the amount of space between two points. It can be measured after an object is pushed or pulled. If one side is stronger, the other group will cross the line farther.

Motion can also be stopped. To do that, an object must be pushed or pulled from the opposite side.

On a swing set, you can drag your toes against the direction of the swing. Then you'll stop. Or your friend can help. Your friend has to pull you back in the opposite direction.

In a soccer game, the ball's motion can be stopped with a foot or a head. Friction between the grass and the ball also slows down or stops motion.

Strength and distance of the push also depends on something else. How fast and how far an object goes depends on weight.

You are pushing your little cousin on a tire swing. He doesn't weigh a lot. He goes higher and faster with each push.

Now your cousin is pushing you. You weigh more than your cousin. It takes more strength to push you. You may not swing as high or as fast.

Weight is also a factor with pulling. It is harder to pull something that is heavy.

You are pulling your friend in a sled. It is hard to pull her up a hill. You have to do a lot of work.

What will happen if your friend gets off the sled? Now the sled is light. You can easily pull it up the hill. It does not take a lot of work.

HOW DOES DIRECTION AFFECT PUSHING AND PULLING?

An object moves in different directions when it's pushed or pulled. It can move up or down. A crane can pull up a piece of cement. You can pull down on a window to close it. When you jump up, your feet push you off the ground.

You can also push and pull an object to the right and left. Pull a rake to the left to grab more leaves. Push a shopping cart right to find the cereal aisle.

The force of a push or a pull may also make the object change direction. **Helium** in balloons pushes them up. But a hand grabbing the strings can pull the balloons down.

A basketball player throws the ball to the right. But a player on the other team can block the ball. Then it goes in a different direction.

A skateboarder heads west on a sidewalk. To turn north, the skateboarder pushes down on the side of the board.

You should be able to predict, or make a good guess about how pushes and pulls affect motion. You make observations and collect **data**. Then you figure out a pattern. How hard does your friend have to push you? How much weight can you pull?

Pushes and pulls are two kinds of forces. Two other kinds of forces are gravity and friction. Forces start, stop, and change motion. Different strength affects motion and its distance. You can affect motion too. Get moving!

GLOSSARY

data (DEY-tuh or DAH-tuh)—facts and information you collect

distance (DIS-tuhns)—the space between two points

force (FORS)—power used on an object

friction (FRIK-shuhn)—a force that stops motion between two things that are touching

gravity (GRAV-i-tee)—a force that pulls everything down toward Earth

helium (HEE-lee-uhm)—a colorless gas used to fill balloons

investigation (in-ves-ti-GEY-shuhn)—a search for information and facts

motion (MOH-shuhn)—the act of changing position; movement

observation (ob-zur-VEY-shuhn)—a note about what is seen or noticed

position (puh-ZISH-uhn)—in reference to a place or location

READ MORE

Cooley Peterson, Megan. *Motion*. Mankato, MN: Pebble, 2019.

Crane, Cody. *Push and Pull*. New York: Children's Press, 2019.

Derting, Kimberly, and Shelli R. Johannes. *Cece Loves Science: Push and Pull*. New York: Greenwillow Books, 2020.

INTERNET SITES

Physics for Kids: Laws of Motion
ducksters.com/science/laws_of_motion.php

Push and Pull: What Kind of Objects Attract to Magnets?
3m.com/3M/en_US/gives-us/education/science-at-home/push-and-pull/

Pushes and Pulls: Hero Elementary
tpt.pbslearningmedia.org/resource/pushes-and-pulls-media-gallery/hero-elementary/

INDEX

ABOUT THE AUTHOR

photo credit: Jillian Raye

Lisa M. Bolt Simons has published more than 45 nonfiction children's books, as well as four middle grade "choose your path" novels and an adult history book. Originally from Colorado, Lisa lives in southern Minnesota with her husband, who also loves to read.